THE SPELL OF THE YUKON

AND OTHER VERSES

BOOKS OF POETRY

By

ROBERT SERVICE

The Spell of the Yukon
Ballads of a Cheechako
Rhymes of a Rolling Stone
Rhymes of a Red Cross Man
Ballads of a Bohemian
The Complete Poems

THE SPELL
OF THE YUKON

By

ROBERT SERVICE

G. P. Putnam's Sons
NEW YORK

ISBN 0-399-15011-0

Printed in the United States of America
10

TO
C. M.

CONTENTS

CONTENTS

CONTENTS

CONTENTS

THE LAND GOD FORGOT

The lonely sunsets flare forlorn
  Down valleys dreadly desolate;
The lordly mountains soar in scorn
  As still as death, as stern as fate.

    The lonely sunsets flame and die;
      The giant valleys gulp the night;
    The monster mountains scrape the sky,
      Where eager stars are diamond-bright.

So gaunt against the gibbous moon,
  Piercing the silence velvet-piled,
A lone wolf howls his ancient rune —
  The fell arch-spirit of the Wild.

    O outcast land! O leper land!
      Let the lone wolf-cry all express
    The hate insensate of thy hand,
      Thy heart's abysmal loneliness.

THE SPELL OF THE YUKON

AND OTHER VERSES

THE SPELL OF THE YUKON

I wanted the gold, and I sought it;
   I scrabbled and mucked like a slave.
Was it famine or scurvy — I fought it;
   I hurled my youth into a grave.
I wanted the gold, and I got it —
   Came out with a fortune last fall,—
Yet somehow life's not what I thought it,
   And somehow the gold isn't all.

No! There's the land. (Have you seen it?)
   It's the cussedest land that I know,
From the big, dizzy mountains that screen it
   To the deep, deathlike valleys below.
Some say God was tired when He made it;
   Some say it's a fine land to shun;
Maybe; but there's some as would trade it
   For no land on earth — and I'm one.

THE SPELL OF THE YUKON

You come to get rich (damned good reason);
    You feel like an exile at first;
You hate it like hell for a season,
    And then you are worse than the worst.
It grips you like some kinds of sinning;
    It twists you from foe to a friend;
It seems it's been since the beginning;
    It seems it will be to the end.

I've stood in some mighty-mouthed hollow
    That's plumb-full of hush to the brim;
I've watched the big, husky sun wallow
    In crimson and gold, and grow dim,
Till the moon set the pearly peaks gleaming,
    And the stars tumbled out, neck and crop;
And I've thought that I surely was dreaming,
    With the peace o' the world piled on top.

The summer — no sweeter was ever;
    The sunshiny woods all athrill;
The grayling aleap in the river,
    The bighorn asleep on the hill.

THE SPELL OF THE YUKON

The strong life that never knows harness;
　The wilds where the caribou call;
The freshness, the freedom, the farness —
　O God! how I'm stuck on it all.

The winter! the brightness that blinds you,
　The white land locked tight as a drum,
The cold fear that follows and finds you,
　The silence that bludgeons you dumb.
The snows that are older than history,
　The woods where the weird shadows slant;
The stillness, the moonlight, the mystery,
　I've bade 'em good-by — but I can't.

There's a land where the mountains are name-
　　less,
　And the rivers all run God knows where;
There are lives that are erring and aimless,
　And deaths that just hang by a hair;
There are hardships that nobody reckons;
　There are valleys unpeopled and still;
There's a land — oh, it beckons and beckons,
　And I want to go back — and I will.

THE SPELL OF THE YUKON

They're making my money diminish;
  I'm sick of the taste of champagne.
Thank God! when I'm skinned to a finish
  I'll pike to the Yukon again.
I'll fight — and you bet it's no sham-fight;
  It's hell! — but I've been there before;
And it's better than this by a damsite —
  So me for the Yukon once more.

There's gold, and it's haunting and haunting;
  It's luring me on as of old;
Yet it isn't the gold that I'm wanting
  So much as just finding the gold.
It's the great, big, broad land 'way up yonder,
  It's the forests where silence has lease;
It's the beauty that thrills me with wonder,
  It's the stillness that fills me with peace.

THE
HEART OF THE SOURDOUGH

There where the mighty mountains bare their
    fangs unto the moon,
There where the sullen sun-dogs glare in the
    snow-bright, bitter noon,
And the glacier-glutted streams sweep down at
    the clarion call of June.

There where the livid tundras keep their tryst
    with the tranquil snows;
There where the silences are spawned, and the
    light of hell-fire flows
Into the bowl of the midnight sky, violet, amber
    and rose.

THE HEART OF THE SOURDOUGH

There where the rapids churn and roar, and the
    ice-floes bellowing run;
Where the tortured, twisted rivers of blood
    rush to the setting sun —
I've packed my kit and I'm going, boys, ere
    another day is done.

       *   *   *   *   *   *

I knew it would call, or soon or late, as it calls
    the whirring wings;
It's the olden lure, it's the golden lure, it's the
    lure of the timeless things,
And to-night, oh, God of the trails untrod, how
    it whines in my heart-strings!

I'm sick to death of your well-groomed gods,
    your make-believe and your show;
I long for a whiff of bacon and beans, a snug
    shakedown in the snow;
A trail to break, and a life at stake, and an-
    other bout with the foe.

THE HEART OF THE SOURDOUGH

With the raw-ribbed Wild that abhors all life,
    the Wild that would crush and rend,
I have clinched and closed with the naked
    North, I have learned to defy and defend;
Shoulder to shoulder we have fought it out —
    yet the Wild must win in the end.

I have flouted the Wild. I have followed its
    lure, fearless, familiar, alone;
By all that the battle means and makes I claim
    that land for mine own;
Yet the Wild must win, and a day will come
    when I shall be overthrown.

Then when as wolf-dogs fight we've fought, the
    lean wolf-land and I;
Fought and bled till the snows are red under
    the reeling sky;
Even as lean wolf-dog goes down will I go
    down and die.

THE THREE VOICES

The waves have a story to tell me,
  As I lie on the lonely beach;
Chanting aloft in the pine-tops,
  The wind has a lesson to teach;
But the stars sing an anthem of glory
  I cannot put into speech.

The waves tell of ocean spaces,
  Of hearts that are wild and brave,
Of populous city places,
  Of desolate shores they lave,
Of men who sally in quest of gold
  To sink in an ocean grave.

The wind is a mighty roamer;
  He bids me keep me free,

THE THREE VOICES

Clean from the taint of the gold-lust,
    Hardy and pure as he;
Cling with my love to nature,
    As a child to the mother-knee.

But the stars throng out in their glory,
    And they sing of the God in man;
They sing of the Mighty Master,
    Of the loom his fingers span,
Where a star or a soul is a part of the whole,
    And weft in the wondrous plan.

Here by the camp-fire's flicker,
    Deep in my blanket curled,
I long for the peace of the pine-gloom,
    When the scroll of the Lord is unfurled,
And the wind and the wave are silent,
    And world is singing to world.

THE LAW OF THE YUKON

This is the law of the Yukon, and ever she
    makes it plain:
" Send not your foolish and feeble; send me
    your strong and your sane —
Strong for the red rage of battle; sane, for I
    harry them sore;
Send me men girt for the combat, men who are
    grit to the core;
Swift as the panther in triumph, fierce as the
    bear in defeat,
Sired of a bulldog parent, steeled in the furnace
    heat.
Send me the best of your breeding, lend me your
    chosen ones;
Them will I take to my bosom, them will I call
    my sons;
Them will I gild with my treasure, them will I
    glut with my meat;

THE LAW OF THE YUKON

But the others — the misfits, the failures — I
    trample under my feet.
Dissolute, damned and despairful, crippled and
    palsied and slain,
Ye would send me the spawn of your gutters —
    Go! take back your spawn again.

" Wild and wide are my borders, stern as death
    is my sway;
From my ruthless throne I have ruled alone for
    a million years and a day;
Hugging my mighty treasure, waiting for man
    to come,
Till he swept like a turbid torrent, and after
    him swept — the scum.
The pallid pimp of the dead-line, the enervate
    of the pen,
One by one I weeded them out, for all that I
    sought was — Men.
One by one I dismayed them, frighting them
    sore with my glooms;
One by one I betrayed them unto my manifold
    dooms.

THE LAW OF THE YUKON

Drowned them like rats in my rivers, starved
    them like curs on my plains,
Rotted the flesh that was left them, poisoned
    the blood in their veins;
Burst with my winter upon them, searing for-
    ever their sight,
Lashed them with fungus-white faces, whimper-
    ing wild in the night;

Staggering blind through the storm-whirl,
    stumbling mad through the snow,
Frozen stiff in the ice-pack, brittle and bent like
    a bow;
Featureless, formless, forsaken, scented by
    wolves in their flight,
Left for the wind to make music through ribs
    that are glittering white;
Gnawing the black crust of failure, searching
    the pit of despair,
Crooking the toe in the trigger, trying to patter
    a prayer;
Going outside with an escort, raving with lips
    all afoam,

THE LAW OF THE YUKON

Writing a cheque for a million, driveling feebly
    of home;
Lost like a louse in the burning . . . or else
    in the tented town
Seeking a drunkard's solace, sinking and sink-
    ing down;
Steeped in the slime at the bottom, dead to a
    decent world,
Lost 'mid the human flotsam, far on the fron-
    tier hurled;
In the camp at the bend of the river, with its
    dozen saloons aglare,
Its gambling dens ariot, its gramophones all
    ablare;
Crimped with the crimes of a city, sin-ridden
    and bridled with lies,
In the hush of my mountained vastness, in the
    flush of my midnight skies.
Plague-spots, yet tools of my purpose, so nathe-
    less I suffer them thrive,
Crushing my Weak in their clutches, that only
    my Strong may survive.

" But the others, the men of my mettle, the men
    who would 'stablish my fame

THE LAW OF THE YUKON

Unto its ultimate issue, winning me honor, not
   shame;
Searching my uttermost valleys, fighting each
   step as they go,
Shooting the wrath of my rapids, scaling my
   ramparts of snow;
Ripping the guts of my mountains, looting the
   beds of my creeks,
Them will I take to my bosom, and speak as a
   mother speaks.
I am the land that listens, I am the land that
   broods;
Steeped in eternal beauty, crystalline waters and
   woods.
Long have I waited lonely, shunned as a thing
   accurst,
Monstrous, moody, pathetic, the last of the
   lands and the first;
Visioning camp-fires at twilight, sad with a long-
   ing forlorn,
Feeling my womb o'er-pregnant with the seed
   of cities unborn.
Wild and wide are my borders, stern as death
   is my sway,

THE LAW OF THE YUKON

And I wait for the men who will win me — and
    I will not be won in a day;
And I will not be won by weaklings, subtle,
    suave and mild,
But by men with the hearts of vikings, and the
    simple faith of a child;
Desperate, strong and resistless, unthrottled by
    fear or defeat,
Them will I gild with my treasure, them will I
    glut with my meat.

" Lofty I stand from each sister land, patient
    and wearily wise,
With the weight of a world of sadness in my
    quiet, passionless eyes;
Dreaming alone of a people, dreaming alone
    of a day,
When men shall not rape my riches, and curse
    me and go away;
Making a bawd of my bounty, fouling the hand
    that gave —
Till I rise in my wrath and I sweep on their
    path and I stamp them into a grave.
Dreaming of men who will bless me, of women
    esteeming me good,

THE LAW OF THE YUKON

Of children born in my borders of radiant
    motherhood,
Of cities leaping to stature, of fame like a flag
    unfurled,
As I pour the tide of my riches in the eager lap
    of the world."

This is the Law of the Yukon, that only the
    Strong shall thrive;
That surely the Weak shall perish, and only the
    Fit survive.
Dissolute, damned and despairful, crippled and
    palsied and slain,
This is the Will of the Yukon,— Lo, how she
    makes it plain!

THE PARSON'S SON

This is the song of the parson's son, as he squats
*   in his shack alone,*
On the wild, weird nights, when the Northern
*   Lights shoot up from the frozen zone,*
And it's sixty below, and couched in the snow
*   the hungry huskies moan:*

" I'm one of the Arctic brotherhood, I'm an
    old-time pioneer.
I came with the first — O God! how I've
    cursed this Yukon — but still I'm here.
I've sweated athirst in its summer heat, I've
    frozen and starved in its cold;
I've followed my dreams by its thousand
    streams, I've toiled and moiled for its gold.

" Look at my eyes — been snow-blind twice;
    look where my foot's half gone;

And that gruesome scar on my left cheek, where
    the frost-fiend bit to the bone.
Each one a brand of this devil's land, where
    I've played and I've lost the game,
A broken wreck with a craze for ' hooch,' and
    never a cent to my name.

" This mining is only a gamble; the worst is as
    good as the best;
I was in with the bunch and I might have come
    out right on top with the rest;
With Cormack, Ladue and Macdonald — O
    God! but it's hell to think
Of the thousands and thousands I've squan-
    dered on cards and women and drink.

" In the early days we were just a few, and we
    hunted and fished around,
Nor dreamt by our lonely camp-fires of the
    wealth that lay under the ground.
We traded in skins and whiskey, and I've often
    slept under the shade
Of that lone birch tree on Bonanza, where the
    first big find was made.

THE PARSON'S SON

"We were just like a great big family, and
    every man had his squaw,
And we lived such a wild, free, fearless life
    beyond the pale of the law;
Till sudden there came a whisper, and it mad-
    dened us every man,
And I got in on Bonanza before the big rush
    began.

"Oh, those Dawson days, and the sin and the
    blaze, and the town all open wide!
(If God made me in His likeness, sure He let
    the devil inside.)
But we all were mad, both the good and the
    bad, and as for the women, well —
No spot on the map in so short a space has
    hustled more souls to hell.

"Money was just like dirt there, easy to get
    and to spend.
I was all caked in on a dance-hall jade, but she
    shook me in the end.

THE PARSON'S SON

It put me queer, and for near a year I never
    drew sober breath,
Till I found myself in the bughouse ward with
    a claim staked out on death.

" Twenty years in the Yukon, struggling along
    its creeks;
Roaming its giant valleys, scaling its god-like
    peaks;
Bathed in its fiery sunsets, fighting its fiendish
    cold —
Twenty years in the Yukon . . . twenty years
    — and I'm old.

" Old and weak, but no matter, there's ' hooch '
    in the bottle still.
I'll hitch up the dogs to-morrow, and mush
    down the trail to Bill.
It's so long dark, and I'm lonesome — I'll just
    lay down on the bed;
To-morrow I'll go . . . to-morrow . . . I
    guess I'll play on the red.

THE PARSON'S SON

" . . . Come, Kit, your pony is saddled.   I'm
      waiting, dear, in the court . . .
. . . Minnie, you devil, I'll kill you if you skip
      with that flossy sport . . .
. . . How much does it go to the pan, Bill? . . .
      play up, School, and play the game . . .
. . . Our Father, which art in heaven, hal-
      lowed be Thy name . . ."

This was the song of the parson's son, as he
      lay in his bunk alone,
Ere the fire went out and the cold crept in, and
      his blue lips ceased to moan,
And the hunger-maddened malamutes had torn
      him flesh from bone.

THE CALL OF THE WILD

Have you gazed on naked grandeur where
there's nothing else to gaze on,
Set pieces and drop-curtain scenes galore,
Big mountains heaved to heaven, which the
blinding sunsets blazon,
Black canyons where the rapids rip and roar?
Have you swept the visioned valley with the
green stream streaking through it,
Searched the Vastness for a something you
have lost?
Have you strung your soul to silence?   Then
for God's sake go and do it;
Hear the challenge, learn the lesson, pay the
cost.

Have you wandered in the wilderness, the sage-
brush desolation,
The bunch-grass levels where the cattle
graze?

THE CALL OF THE WILD

Have you whistled bits of rag-time at the end
    of all creation,
  And learned to know the desert's little
    ways?
Have you camped upon the foothills, have you
    galloped o'er the ranges,
  Have you roamed the arid sun-lands through
    and through?
Have you chummed up with the mesa? Do
    you know its moods and changes?
  Then listen to the Wild — it's calling you.

Have you known the Great White Silence, not
    a snow-gemmed twig aquiver?
  (Eternal truths that shame our soothing
    lies.)
Have you broken trail on snowshoes? mushed
    your huskies up the river,
  Dared the unknown, led the way, and
    clutched the prize?
Have you marked the map's void spaces,
    mingled with the mongrel races,
  Felt the savage strength of brute in every
    thew?

THE CALL OF THE WILD

And though grim as hell the worst is, can you
    round it off with curses?
  Then hearken to the Wild — it's wanting
    you.

Have you suffered, starved and triumphed,
    groveled down, yet grasped at glory,
  Grown bigger in the bigness of the whole?
" Done things " just for the doing, letting bab-
    blers tell the story,
  Seeing through the nice veneer the naked
    soul?
Have you seen God in His splendors, heard the
    text that nature renders?
  (You'll never hear it in the family pew.)
The simple things, the true things, the silent
    men who do things —
  Then listen to the Wild — it's calling you.

They have cradled you in custom, they have
    primed you with their preaching,
  They have soaked you in convention through
    and through;
They have put you in a showcase; you're a
    credit to their teaching —

THE CALL OF THE WILD

But can't you hear the Wild? — it's calling
you.
Let us probe the silent places, let us seek what
luck betide us;
Let us journey to a lonely land I know.
There's a whisper on the night-wind, there's
a star agleam to guide us,
And the Wild is calling, calling . . . let us
go.

THE LONE TRAIL

*Ye who know the Lone Trail fain would follow
it,*
*Though it lead to glory or the darkness of the
pit.*
*Ye who take the Lone Trail, bid your love
good-by;*
*The Lone Trail, the Lone Trail follow till you
die.*

The trails of the world be countless, and most
of the trails be tried;
You tread on the heels of the many, till you
come where the ways divide;
And one lies safe in the sunlight, and the other
is dreary and wan,
Yet you look aslant at the Lone Trail, and the
Lone Trail lures you on.
And somehow you're sick of the highway, with
its noise and its easy needs,
And you seek the risk of the by-way, and you
reck not where it leads.

THE LONE TRAIL

And sometimes it leads to the desert, and the
    tongue swells out of the mouth,
And you stagger blind to the mirage, to die in
    the mocking drouth.
And sometimes it leads to the mountain, to the
    light of the lone camp-fire,
And you gnaw your belt in the anguish of
    hunger-goaded desire.
And sometimes it leads to the Southland, to the
    swamp where the orchid glows,
And you rave to your grave with the fever, and
    they rob the corpse for its clothes.
And sometimes it leads to the Northland, and
    the scurvy softens your bones,
And your flesh dints in like putty, and you spit
    out your teeth like stones.
And sometimes it leads to a coral reef in the
    wash of a weedy sea,
And you sit and stare at the empty glare where
    the gulls wait greedily.
And sometimes it leads to an Arctic trail,
    and the snows where your torn feet
    freeze,
And you whittle away the useless clay, and
    crawl on your hands and knees.

THE LONE TRAIL

Often it leads to the dead-pit; always it leads
    to pain;
By the bones of your brothers ye know it, but
    oh, to follow you're fain.
By your bones they will follow behind you, till
    the ways of the world are made plain.

*Bid good-by to sweetheart, bid good-by to
    friend;*
*The Lone Trail, the Lone Trail follow to the
    end.*
Tarry not, and fear not, chosen of the true;
*Lover of the Lone Trail, the Lone Trail waits
    for you.*

THE PINES

We sleep in the sleep of ages, the bleak, bar-
    barian pines;
The gray moss drapes us like sages, and closer
    we lock our lines,
And deeper we clutch through the gelid gloom
    where never a sunbeam shines.

On the flanks of the storm-gored ridges are our
    black battalions massed;
We surge in a host to the sullen coast, and we
    sing in the ocean blast;
From empire of sea to empire of snow we grip
    our empire fast.

To the niggard lands were we driven, 'twixt
    desert and floes are we penned;
To us was the Northland given, ours to strong-
    hold and defend;

THE PINES

Ours till the world be riven in the crash of the
  utter end;

Ours from the bleak beginning, through the
  æons of death-like sleep;
Ours from the shock when the naked rock was
  hurled from the hissing deep;
Ours through the twilight ages of weary glacier
  creep.

Wind of the East, Wind of the West, wander-
  ing to and fro,
Chant your songs in our topmost boughs, that
  the sons of men may know
The peerless pine was the first to come, and the
  pine will be last to go!

We pillar the halls of perfumed gloom; we
  plume where the eagles soar;
The North-wind swoops from the brooding
  Pole, and our ancients crash and roar;
But where one falls from the crumbling walls
  shoots up a hardy score.

44

THE PINES

We spring from the gloom of the canyon's
    womb; in the valley's lap we lie;
From the white foam-fringe, where the break-
    ers cringe to the peaks that tusk the sky,
We climb, and we peer in the crag-locked mere
    that gleams like a golden eye.

Gain to the verge of the hog-back ridge where
    the vision ranges free:
Pines and pines and the shadow of pines as far
    as the eye can see;
A steadfast legion of stalwart knights in domi-
    nant empery.

Sun, moon and stars give answer; shall we not
    staunchly stand,
Even as now, forever, wards of the wilder
    strand,
Sentinels of the stillness, lords of the last, lone
    land?

THE LURE OF LITTLE VOICES

There's a cry from out the loneliness — oh,
    listen, Honey, listen!
  Do you hear it, do you fear it, you're a-hold-
      ing of me so?
You're a-sobbing in your sleep, dear, and your
    lashes, how they glisten —
  Do you hear the Little Voices all a-begging
      me to go?

All a-begging me to leave you.　Day and night
    they're pleading, praying,
  On the North-wind, on the West-wind, from
      the peak and from the plain;
Night and day they never leave me — do you
    know what they are saying?
  "He was ours before you got him, and we
      want him once again."

THE LURE OF LITTLE VOICES

Yes, they're wanting me, they're haunting me,
    the awful lonely places;
  They're whining and they're whimpering as
    if each had a soul;
They're calling from the wilderness, the vast
    and God-like spaces,
  The stark and sullen solitudes that sentinel
    the Pole.

They miss my little camp-fires, ever brightly,
    bravely gleaming
  In the womb of desolation, where was never
    man before;
As comradeless I sought them, lion-hearted,
    loving, dreaming,
  And they hailed me as a comrade, and they
    loved me evermore.

And now they're all a-crying, and it's no use me
    denying;
  The spell of them is on me and I'm helpless
    as a child;

THE LURE OF LITTLE VOICES

My heart is aching, aching, but I hear them,
   sleeping, waking;
   It's the Lure of Little Voices, it's the man-
      date of the Wild.

I'm afraid to tell you, Honey, I can take no
      bitter leaving;
   But softly in the sleep-time from your love
      I'll steal away.
Oh, it's cruel, dearie, cruel, and it's God knows
      how I'm grieving;
   But His loneliness is calling, and He knows
      I must obey.

THE SONG OF THE WAGE-SLAVE

When the long, long day is over, and the Big
Boss gives me my pay,
I hope that it won't be hell-fire, as some of the
parsons say.
And I hope that it won't be heaven, with some
of the parsons I've met —
All I want is just quiet, just to rest and forget.
Look at my face, toil-furrowed; look at my
calloused hands;
Master, I've done Thy bidding, wrought in Thy
many lands —
Wrought for the little masters, big-bellied they
be, and rich;
I've done their desire for a daily hire, and I die
like a dog in a ditch.
I have used the strength Thou hast given, Thou
knowest I did not shirk;
Threescore years of labor — Thine be the long
day's work.

THE SONG OF THE WAGE-SLAVE

And now, Big Master, I'm broken and bent and
   twisted and scarred,
But I've held my job, and Thou knowest, and
   Thou will not judge me hard.
Thou knowest my sins are many, and often I've
   played the fool —
Whiskey and cards and women, they made me
   the devil's tool.
I was just like a child with money; I flung it
   away with a curse,
Feasting a fawning parasite, or glutting a har-
   lot's purse;
Then back to the woods repentant, back to the
   mill or the mine,
I, the worker of workers, everything in my line.
Everything hard but headwork (I'd no more
   brains than a kid),
A brute with brute strength to labor, doing as
   I was bid;
Living in camps with men-folk, a lonely and
   loveless life;
Never knew kiss of sweetheart, never caress of
   wife.
A brute with brute strength to labor, and they
   were so far above —

THE SONG OF THE WAGE-SLAVE

Yet I'd gladly have gone to the gallows for one
    little look of Love.

I, with the strength of two men, savage and shy
    and wild —

Yet how I'd ha' treasured a woman, and the
    sweet, warm kiss of a child!

Well, 'tis Thy world, and Thou knowest. I
    blaspheme and my ways be rude;

But I've lived my life as I found it, and I've
    done my best to be good;

I, the primitive toiler, half naked and grimed
    to the eyes,

Sweating it deep in their ditches, swining it
    stark in their styes;

Hurling down forests before me, spanning tu-
    multuous streams;

Down in the ditch building o'er me palaces
    fairer than dreams;

Boring the rock to the ore-bed, driving the road
    through the fen,

Resolute, dumb, uncomplaining, a man in a
    world of men.

Master, I've filled my contract, wrought in Thy
    many lands;

THE SONG OF THE WAGE-SLAVE

Not by my sins wilt Thou judge me, but by the
    work of my hands.
Master, I've done Thy bidding, and the light is
    low in the west,
And the long, long shift is over . . . Master,
    I've earned it — Rest.

GRIN

If you're up against a bruiser and you're get-
    ting knocked about —
                 Grin.
If you're feeling pretty groggy, and you're
    licked beyond a doubt —
                 Grin.
Don't let him see you're funking, let him know
    with every clout,
Though your face is battered to a pulp, your
    blooming heart is stout;
Just stand upon your pins until the beggar
    knocks you out —
             And grin.
This life's a bally battle, and the same advice
    holds true
             Of grin.
If you're up against it badly, then it's only one
    on you,
             So grin.

GRIN

If the future's black as thunder, don't let people
    see you're blue;
Just cultivate a cast-iron smile of joy the whole
    day through;
If they call you " Little Sunshine," wish that
    they'd no troubles, too —

                You may — grin.
Rise up in the morning with the will that,
    smooth or rough,

                You'll grin.
Sink to sleep at midnight, and although you're
    feeling tough,

                Yet grin.
There's nothing gained by whining, and you're
    not that kind of stuff;
You're a fighter from away back, and you *won't*
    take a rebuff;
Your trouble is that you don't know when you
    have had enough —

                Don't give in.
If Fate should down you, just get up and take
    another cuff;
You may bank on it that there is no philosophy
    like bluff,

                And grin.

THE SHOOTING OF DAN McGREW

A bunch of the boys were whooping it up in the
    Malamute saloon;
The kid that handles the music-box was hitting
    a jag-time tune;
Back of the bar, in a solo game, sat Dangerous
    Dan McGrew,
And watching his luck was his light-o'-love, the
    lady that's known as Lou.

When out of the night, which was fifty below,
    and into the din and the glare,
There stumbled a miner fresh from the creeks,
    dog-dirty, and loaded for bear.
He looked like a man with a foot in the grave
    and scarcely the strength of a louse,
Yet he tilted a poke of dust on the bar, and he
    called for drinks for the house.

THE SHOOTING OF DAN McGREW

There was none could place the stranger's face,
though we searched ourselves for a clue;
But we drank his health, and the last to drink
was Dangerous Dan McGrew.

There's men that somehow just grip your eyes,
and hold them hard like a spell;
And such was he, and he looked to me like a
man who had lived in hell;
With a face most hair, and the dreary stare of
a dog whose day is done,
As he watered the green stuff in his glass, and
the drops fell one by one.
Then I got to figgering who he was, and won-
dering what he'd do,
And I turned my head — and there watching
him was the lady that's known as Lou.

His eyes went rubbering round the room, and
he seemed in a kind of daze,
Till at last that old piano fell in the way of his
wandering gaze.

THE SHOOTING OF DAN McGREW

The rag-time kid was having a drink; there
    was no one else on the stool,
So the stranger stumbles across the room, and
    flops down there like a fool.
In a buckskin shirt that was glazed with dirt
    he sat, and I saw him sway;
Then he clutched the keys with his talon hands
    — my God! but that man could play.

Were you ever out in the Great Alone, when the
    moon was awful clear,
And the icy mountains hemmed you in with a
    silence you most could *hear;*
With only the howl of a timber wolf, and you
    camped there in the cold,
A half-dead thing in a stark, dead world, clean
    mad for the muck called gold;
While high overhead, green, yellow and red,
    the North Lights swept in bars? —
Then you've a haunch what the music meant
    . . . hunger and night and the stars.

And hunger not of the belly kind, that's ban-
    ished with bacon and beans,

But the gnawing hunger of lonely men for a
 home and all that it means;
For a fireside far from the cares that are, four
 walls and a roof above;
But oh! so cramful of cosy joy, and crowned
 with a woman's love —
A woman dearer than all the world, and true
 as Heaven is true —
(God! how ghastly she looks through her
 rouge,— the lady that's known as Lou.)

Then on a sudden the music changed, so soft
 that you scarce could hear;
But you felt that your life had been looted clean
 of all that it once held dear;
That someone had stolen the woman you loved;
 that her love was a devil's lie;
That your guts were gone, and the best for you
 was to crawl away and die.
'Twas the crowning cry of a heart's despair,
 and it thrilled you through and through —
" I guess I'll make it a spread misere," said
 Dangerous Dan McGrew.

58

THE SHOOTING OF DAN McGREW

The music almost died away . . . then it burst
    like a pent-up flood;
And it seemed to say, " Repay, repay," and my
    eyes were blind with blood.
The thought came back of an ancient wrong,
    and it stung like a frozen lash,
And the lust awoke to kill, to kill . . . then
    the music stopped with a crash,
And the stranger turned, and his eyes they
    burned in a most peculiar way;
In a buckskin shirt that was glazed with dirt
    he sat, and I saw him sway;
Then his lips went in in a kind of grin, and he
    spoke, and his voice was calm,
And " Boys," says he, " you don't know me,
    and none of you care a damn;
But I want to state, and my words are straight,
    and I'll bet my poke they're true,
That one of you is a hound of hell . . . and
    that one is Dan McGrew."

Then I ducked my head, and the lights went
    out, and two guns blazed in the dark,

THE SHOOTING OF DAN McGREW

And a woman screamed, and the lights went up,
    and two men lay stiff and stark.
Pitched on his head, and pumped full of lead,
    was Dangerous Dan MGrew,
While the man from the creeks lay clutched to
    the breast of the lady that's known as Lou.

These are the simple facts of the case, and I
    guess I ought to know.
They say that the stranger was crazed with
    " hooch," and I'm not denying it's so.
I'm not so wise as the lawyer guys, but strictly
    between us two —
The woman that kissed him and — pinched his
    poke — was the lady that's known as Lou.

THE CREMATION OF SAM McGEE

There are strange things done in the midnight
    sun
  By the men who moil for gold;
The Arctic trails have their secret tales
  That would make your blood run cold;
The Northern Lights have seen queer sights,
  But the queerest they ever did see
Was that night on the marge of Lake Lebarge
  I cremated Sam McGee.

Now Sam McGee was from Tennessee, where
    the cotton blooms and blows.
Why he left his home in the South to roam
    'round the Pole, God only knows.
He was always cold, but the land of gold seemed
    to hold him like a spell;
Though he'd often say in his homely way that
    " he'd sooner live in hell."

THE CREMATION OF SAM McGEE

On a Christmas Day we were mushing our way
    over the Dawson trail.
Talk of your cold! through the parka's fold it
    stabbed like a driven nail.
If our eyes we'd close, then the lashes froze till
    sometimes we couldn't see;
It wasn't much fun, but the only one to whimper
    was Sam McGee.

And that very night, as we lay packed tight in
    our robes beneath the snow,
And the dogs were fed, and the stars o'erhead
    were dancing heel and toe,
He turned to me, and " Cap," says he, " I'll cash
    in this trip, I guess;
And if I do, I'm asking that you won't refuse my
    last request."

Well, he seemed so low that I couldn't say no;
    then he says with a sort of moan:
" It's the cursèd cold, and it's got right hold till
    I'm chilled clean through to the bone.

THE CREMATION OF SAM McGEE

Yet 'tain't being dead — it's my awful dread of
    the icy grave that pains;
So I want you to swear that, foul or fair, you'll
    cremate my last remains."

A pal's last need is a thing to heed, so I swore
    I would not fail;
And we started on at the streak of dawn; but
    God! he looked ghastly pale.
He crouched on the sleigh, and he raved all day
    of his home in Tennessee;
And before nightfall a corpse was all that was
    left of Sam McGee.

There wasn't a breath in that land of death, and
    I hurried, horror-driven,
With a corpse half hid that I couldn't get rid,
    because of a promise given;
It was lashed to the sleigh, and it seemed to say:
    " You may tax your brawn and brains,
But you promised true, and it's up to you to
    cremate those last remains."

THE CREMATION OF SAM McGEE

Now a promise made is a debt unpaid, and the
    trail has its own stern code.
In the days to come, though my lips were dumb,
    in my heart how I cursed that load.
In the long, long night, by the lone firelight,
    while the huskies, round in a ring,
Howled out their woes to the homeless snows
    — O God! how I loathed the thing.

And every day that quiet clay seemed to heavy
    and heavier grow;
And on I went, though the dogs were spent and
    the grub was getting low;
The trail was bad, and I felt half mad, but I
    swore I would not give in;
And I'd often sing to the hateful thing, and it
    hearkened with a grin.

Till I came to the marge of Lake Lebarge, and
    a derelict there lay;
It was jammed in the ice, but I saw in a trice it
    was called the " Alice May."

64

THE CREMATION OF SAM McGEE

And I looked at it, and I thought a bit, and I
    looked at my frozen chum;
Then "Here," said I, with a sudden cry, "is
    my cre-ma-tor-eum."

Some planks I tore from the cabin floor, and I
    lit the boiler fire;
Some coal I found that was lying around, and I
    heaped the fuel higher;
The flames just soared, and the furnace roared
    — such a blaze you seldom see;
And I burrowed a hole in the glowing coal, and
    I stuffed in Sam McGee.

Then I made a hike, for I didn't like to hear him
    sizzle so;
And the heavens scowled, and the huskies
    howled, and the wind began to blow.
It was icy cold, but the hot sweat rolled down my
    cheeks, and I don't know why;
And the greasy smoke in an inky cloak went
    streaking down the sky.

THE CREMATION OF SAM McGEE

I do not know how long in the snow I wrestled
    with grisly fear;
But the stars came out and they danced about
    ere again I ventured near;
I was sick with dread, but I bravely said: " I'll
    just take a peep inside.
I guess he's cooked, and it's time I looked "; . . .
    then the door I opened wide.

And there sat Sam, looking cool and calm, in the
    heart of the furnace roar;
And he wore a smile you could see a mile, and
    he said: " Please close that door.
It's fine in here, but I greatly fear you'll let in
    the cold and storm —
Since I left Plumtree, down in Tennessee, it's
    the first time I've been warm."

There are strange things done in the midnight sun
    By the men who moil for gold;
The Arctic trails have their secret tales
    That would make your blood run cold;

THE CREMATION OF SAM McGEE

The Northern Lights have seen queer sights,
  But the queerest they ever did see
Was that night on the marge of Lake Lebarge
  I cremated Sam McGee.

MY MADONNA

I haled me a woman from the street,
  Shameless, but, oh, so fair!
I bade her sit in the model's seat
  And I painted her sitting there.

I hid all trace of her heart unclean;
  I painted a babe at her breast;
I painted her as she might have been
  If the Worst had been the Best.

She laughed at my picture and went away.
  Then came, with a knowing nod,
A connoisseur, and I heard him say;
  " 'Tis Mary, the Mother of God."

So I painted a halo round her hair,
  And I sold her and took my fee,
And she hangs in the church of Saint Hillaire,
  Where you and all may see.

68

UNFORGOTTEN

I know a garden where the lilies gleam,
   And one who lingers in the sunshine there;
   She is than white-stoled lily far more fair,
And oh, her eyes are heaven-lit with dream!

I know a garret, cold and dark and drear,
   And one who toils and toils with tireless pen,
   Until his brave, sad eyes grow weary — then
He seeks the stars, pale, silent as a seer.

And ah, it's strange; for, desolate and dim,
   Between these two there rolls an ocean wide;
   Yet he is in the garden by her side
And she is in the garret there with him.

THE RECKONING

It's fine to have a blow-out in a fancy restau-
    rant,
With terrapin and canvas-back and all the wine
    you want;
To enjoy the flowers and music, watch the
    pretty women pass,
Smoke a choice cigar, and sip the wealthy
    water in your glass.
It's bully in a high-toned joint to eat and drink
    your fill,
But it's quite another matter when you
                  Pay the bill.

It's great to go out every night on fun or
    pleasure bent;
To wear your glad rags always and to never
    save a cent;

THE RECKONING

To drift along regardless, have a good time
 every trip;
To hit the high spots sometimes, and to let your
 chances slip;
To know you're acting foolish, yet to go on
 fooling still,
Till Nature calls a show-down, and you
       Pay the bill.

Time has got a little bill — get wise while yet
 you may,
For the debit side's increasing in a most alarm-
 ing way;
The things you had no right to do, the things
 you should have done,
They're all put down; it's up to you to pay for
 every one.
So eat, drink and be merry, have a good time
 if you will,
But God help you when the time comes, and you
       Foot the bill.

QUATRAINS

One said: Thy life is thine to make or mar,
To flicker feebly, or to soar, a star;
    It lies with thee — the choice is thine, is thine,
To hit the ties or drive thy auto-car.

I answered Her: The choice is mine — ah, no!
We all were made or marred long, long ago.
    The parts are written; hear the super wail:
" Who is stage-managing this cosmic show? "

Blind fools of fate and slaves of circumstance,
Life is a fiddler, and we all must dance.
    From gloom where mocks that will-o'-wisp, Free-will
I heard a voice cry: " Say, give us a chance."

QUATRAINS

Chance! Oh, there is no chance! The scene
    is set.
Up with the curtain! Man, the marionette,
    Resumes his part. The gods will work the
      wires.
They've got it all down fine, you bet, you bet!

It's all decreed — the mighty earthquake crash;
The countless constellations' wheel and flash;
    The rise and fall of empires, war's red tide;
The composition of your dinner hash.

There's no haphazard in this world of ours.
Cause and effect are grim, relentless powers.
    They rule the world. (A king was shot last
      night;
Last night I held the joker and both bowers.)

From out the mesh of fate our heads we thrust.
We can't do what we would, but what we must.
    Heredity has got us in a cinch —
(Consoling thought when you've been on a
      " bust.")

QUATRAINS

Hark to the song where spheral voices blend:
" There's no beginning, never will be end."
   It makes us nutty; hang the astral chimes!
The tables spread; come, let us dine, my friend.

THE MEN THAT DON'T FIT IN

There's a race of men that don't fit in,
    A race that can't stay still;
So they break the hearts of kith and kin,
    And they roam the world at will.
They range the field and they rove the flood,
    And they climb the mountain's crest;
Theirs is the curse of the gypsy blood,
    And they don't know how to rest.

If they just went straight they might go far;
    They are strong and brave and true;
But they're always tired of the things that are,
    And they want the strange and new.
They say: " Could I find my proper groove,
    What a deep mark I would make ! "
So they chop and change, and each fresh move
    Is only a fresh mistake.

THE MEN THAT DON'T FIT IN

And each forgets, as he strips and runs
  With a brilliant, fitful pace,
It's the steady, quiet, plodding ones
  Who win in the lifelong race.
And each forgets that his youth has fled,
  Forgets that his prime is past,
Till he stands one day, with a hope that's dead,
  In the glare of the truth at last.

He has failed, he has failed; he has missed his
      chance;
  He has just done things by half.
Life's been a jolly good joke on him,
  And now is the time to laugh.
Ha, ha! He is one of the Legion Lost;
  He was never meant to win;
He's a rolling stone, and it's bred in the bone;
  He's a man who won't fit in.

MUSIC IN THE BUSH

O'er the dark pines she sees the silver moon,
    And in the west, all tremulous, a star;
And soothing sweet she hears the mellow tune
    Of cow-bells jangled in the fields afar.

Quite listless, for her daily stent is done,
    She stands, sad exile, at her rose-wreathed
        door,
And sends her love eternal with the sun
    That goes to gild the land she'll see no more.

The grave, gaunt pines imprison her sad gaze,
    All still the sky and darkling drearily;
She feels the chilly breath of dear, dead days
    Come sifting through the alders eerily.

MUSIC IN THE BUSH

Oh, how the roses riot in their bloom!
  The curtains stir as with an ancient pain;
Her old piano gleams from out the gloom
  And waits and waits her tender touch in vain.

But now her hands like moonlight brush the keys
  With velvet grace — melodious delight;
And now a sad refrain from over seas
  Goes sobbing on the bosom of the night;

And now she sings.   (O! singer in the gloom,
  Voicing a sorrow we can ne'er express,
Here in the Farness where we few have room
  Unshamed to show our love and tenderness,

Our hearts will echo, till they beat no more,
  That song of sadness and of motherland;
And, stretched in deathless love to England's
      shore,
  Some day she'll hearken and she'll under-
    stand.)

MUSIC IN THE BUSH

A prima-donna in the shining past,
  But now a mother growing old and gray,
She thinks of how she held a people fast
  In thrall, and gleaned the triumphs of a day.

She sees a sea of faces like a dream;
  She sees herself a queen of song once more;
She sees lips part in rapture, eyes agleam;
  She sings as never once she sang before.

She sings a wild, sweet song that throbs with
      pain,
  The added pain of life that transcends art —
A song of home, a deep, celestial strain,
  The glorious swan-song of a dying heart.

A lame tramp comes along the railway track,
  A grizzled dog whose day is nearly done;
He passes, pauses, then comes slowly back
  And listens there — an audience of one.

MUSIC IN THE BUSH

She sings — her golden voice is passion-fraught,
    As when she charmed a thousand eager ears;
He listens trembling, and she knows it not,
    And down his hollow cheeks roll bitter tears.

She ceases and is still, as if to pray;
    There is no sound, the stars are all alight —
Only a wretch who stumbles on his way,
    Only a vagrant sobbing in the night.

THE RHYME OF THE REMIT-
TANCE MAN

There's a four-pronged buck a-swinging in the
    shadow of my cabin,
  And it roamed the velvet valley till to-day;
But I tracked it by the river, and I trailed it in
    the cover,
  And I killed it on the mountain miles away.
Now I've had my lazy supper, and the level
    sun is gleaming
  On the water where the silver salmon play;
And I light my little corn-cob, and I linger,
    softly dreaming,
  In the twilight, of a land that's far away.

Far away, so faint and far, is flaming London,
    fevered Paris,
  That I fancy I have gained another star;

RHYME OF THE REMITTANCE MAN

Far away the din and hurry, far away the sin
    and worry,
    Far away — God knows they cannot be too
      far.
Gilded galley-slaves of Mammon — how my
    purse-proud brothers taunt me!
    I might have been as well-to-do as they
Had I clutched like them my chances,
    learned their wisdom, crushed my
    fancies,
    Starved my soul and gone to business every
    day.

Well, the cherry bends with blossom and the
    vivid grass is springing,
    And the star-like lily nestles in the
    green;
And the frogs their joys are singing, and my
    heart in tune is ringing,
    And it doesn't matter what I might have
    been.
While above the scented pine-gloom, piling
    heights of golden glory,
    The sun-god paints his canvas in the west,

RHYME OF THE REMITTANCE MAN

I can couch me deep in clover, I can listen to
    the story
  Of the lazy, lapping water — it is best.

While the trout leaps in the river, and the blue
    grouse thrills the cover,
  And the frozen snow betrays the panther's
    track,
And the robin greets the dayspring with the
    rapture of a lover,
  I am happy, and I'll nevermore go back.
For I know I'd just be longing for the little old
    log cabin,
  With the morning-glory clinging to the door,
Till I loathed the city places, cursed the care
    on all the faces,
  Turned my back on lazar London evermore.

So send me far from Lombard Street, and write
    me down a failure;
  Put a little in my purse and leave me free.
Say: " He turned from Fortune's offering to
    follow up a pale lure,
  He is one of us no longer — let him be."

RHYME OF THE REMITTANCE MAN

I am one of you no longer; by the trails my feet
    have broken,
  The dizzy peaks I've scaled, the camp-fire's
    glow;
By the lonely seas I've sailed in — yea, the final
    word is spoken,
  I am signed and sealed to nature. Be it so.

THE LOW-DOWN WHITE

This is the pay-day up at the mines, when the
    bearded brutes come down;
There's money to burn in the streets to-night,
    so I've sent my klooch to town,
With a haggard face and a ribband of red en-
    twined in her hair of brown.

And I know at the dawn she'll come reeling
    home with the bottles, one, two, three —
One for herself, to drown her shame, and two
    big bottles for me,
To make me forget the thing I am and the man
    I used to be.

THE LOW-DOWN WHITE

To make me forget the brand of the dog, as I
 crouch in this hideous place;
To make me forget once I kindled the light of
 love in a lady's face,
Where even the squalid Siwash now holds me
 a black disgrace.

Oh, I have guarded my secret well!   And who
 would dream as I speak
In a tribal tongue like a rogue unhung, 'mid the
 ranch-house filth and reek,
I could roll to bed with a Latin phrase and rise
 with a verse of Greek?

Yet I was a senior prizeman once, and the pride
 of a college eight;
Called to the bar — my friends were true! but
 they could not keep me straight;
Then came the divorce, and I went abroad and
 " died " on the River Plate.

THE LOW-DOWN WHITE

But I'm not dead yet; though with half a lung
    there isn't time to spare,
And I hope that the year will see me out, and,
    thank God, no one will care —
Save maybe the little slim Siwash girl with the
    rose of shame in her hair.

She will come with the dawn, and the dawn is
    near; I can see its evil glow,
Like a corpse-light seen through a frosty pane
    in a night of want and woe;
And yonder she comes by the bleak bull-pines,
    swift staggering through the snow.

THE LITTLE OLD LOG CABIN

When a man gits on his uppers in a hard-pan
    sort of town,
    An' he ain't got nothin' comin' an' he can't
        afford ter eat,
An' he's in a fix for lodgin' an' he wanders up
    an' down,
    An' you'd fancy he'd been boozin', he's so
        locoed 'bout the feet;
When he's feelin' sneakin' sorry an' his belt is
    hangin' slack,
    An' his face is peaked an' gray-like an' his
        heart gits down an' whines,
Then he's apt ter git a-thinkin' an' a-wishin' he
    was back
    In the little ol' log cabin in the shadder of
        the pines.

THE LITTLE OLD LOG CABIN

When he's on the blazin' desert an' his canteen's
    sprung a leak,
  An' he's all alone an' crazy an' he's crawlin'
    like a snail,
An' his tongue's so black an' swollen that it
    hurts him fer to speak,
  An' he gouges down fer water an' the raven's
    on his trail;
When he's done with care and cursin' an' he
    feels more like to cry,
  An' he sees ol' Death a-grinnin' an' he thinks
    upon his crimes,
Then he's like ter hev' a vision, as he settles
    down ter die,
  Of the little ol' log cabin an' the roses an'
    the vines.

Oh, the little ol' log cabin, it's a solemn shinin'
    mark,
  When a feller gits ter sinnin' an' a-goin' ter
    the wall,
An' folks don't understand him an' he's gropin'
    in the dark,

THE LITTLE OLD LOG CABIN

An' he's sick of bein' cursed at an' he's
    longin' fer his call!
When the sun of life's a-sinkin' you can see it
    'way above,
  On the hill from out the shadder in a glory
      'gin the sky,
An' your mother's voice is callin', an' her arms
    are stretched in love,
  An' somehow you're glad you're goin', an'
      you ain't a-scared to die;
When you'll be like a kid again an' nestle to
    her breast,
An' never leave its shelter, an' forget, an' love,
    an' rest.

THE YOUNGER SON

If you leave the gloom of London and you seek
    a glowing land,
    Where all except the flag is strange and new,
There's a bronzed and stalwart fellow who will
    grip you by the hand,
    And greet you with a welcome warm and
    true;
For he's your younger brother, the one you
    sent away
    Because there wasn't room for him at home;
And now he's quite contented, and he's glad he
    didn't stay,
    And he's building Britain's greatness o'er the
    foam.

When the giant herd is moving at the rising of
    the sun,
    And the prairie is lit with rose and gold,

THE YOUNGER SON

And the camp is all abustle, and the busy day's
    begun,
  He leaps into the saddle sure and bold.
Through the round of heat and hurry, through
    the racket and the rout,
  He rattles at a pace that nothing mars;
And when the night-winds whisper and camp-
    fires flicker out,
  He is sleeping like a child beneath the stars.

When the wattle-blooms are drooping in the
    sombre shed-oak glade,
  And the breathless land is lying in a swoon,
He leaves his work a moment, leaning lightly
    on his spade,
  And he hears the bell-bird chime the Austral
    noon.
The parrakeets are silent in the gum-tree by the
    creek;
  The ferny grove is sunshine-steeped and
    still;
But the dew will gem the myrtle in the twilight
    ere he seek
  His little lonely cabin on the hill.

THE YOUNGER SON

Around the purple, vine-clad slope the argent
    river dreams;
  The roses almost hide the house from view;
A snow-peak of the Winterberg in crimson
    splendor gleams;
  The shadow deepens down on the karroo.
He seeks the lily-scented dusk beneath the
    orange tree;
  His pipe in silence glows and fades and
    glows;
And then two little maids come out and climb
    upon his knee,
  And one is like the lily, one the rose.

He sees his white sheep dapple o'er the green
    New Zealand plain,
  And where Vancouver's shaggy ramparts
    frown,
When the sunlight threads the pine-gloom he is
    fighting might and main
  To clinch the rivets of an Empire down.
You will find him toiling, toiling, in the south
    or in the west,
  A child of nature, fearless, frank and free;

THE YOUNGER SON

And the warmest heart that beats for you is
 beating in his breast,
 And he sends you loyal greeting o'er the sea.

You've a brother in the army, you've another in
 the Church;
 One of you is a diplomatic swell;
You've had the pick of everything and left him
 in the lurch,
 And yet I think he's doing very well.
I'm sure his life is happy, and he doesn't envy
 yours;
 I know he loves the land his pluck has won;
And I fancy in the years unborn, while Eng-
 land's fame endures,
 She will come to bless with pride — The
 Younger Son.

THE MARCH OF THE DEAD

The cruel war was over — oh, the triumph was
    so sweet!
  We watched the troops returning, through
    our tears;
There was triumph, triumph, triumph down the
    scarlet glittering street,
  And you scarce could hear the music for the
    cheers.
And you scarce could see the house-tops for the
    flags that flew between;
  The bells were pealing madly to the sky;
And everyone was shouting for the Soldiers of
    the Queen,
  And the glory of an age was passing by.

And then there came a shadow, swift and sud-
    den, dark and drear;
  The bells were silent, not an echo stirred.

95

THE MARCH OF THE DEAD

The flags were drooping sullenly, the men for-
      got to cheer;
  We waited, and we never spoke a word.
The sky grew darker, darker, till from out the
      gloomy rack
  There came a voice that checked the heart
      with dread:
" Tear down, tear down your bunting now, and
      hang up sable black;
  They are coming — it's the Army of the
      Dead."

They were coming, they were coming, gaunt and
      ghastly, sad and slow;
  They were coming, all the crimson wrecks of
      pride;
With faces seared, and cheeks red smeared, and
      haunting eyes of woe,
  And clotted holes the khaki couldn't hide.
Oh, the clammy brow of anguish! the livid,
      foam-flecked lips!
  The reeling ranks of ruin swept along!
The limb that trailed, the hand that failed, the
      bloody finger tips!
  And oh, the dreary rhythm of their song!

THE MARCH OF THE DEAD

" They left us on the veldt-side, but we felt we
    couldn't stop
  On this, our England's crowning festal day;
We're the men of Magersfontein, we're the men
    of Spion Kop,
  Colenso — we're the men who had to pay.
We're the men who paid the blood-price.   Shall
    the grave be all our gain?
  You owe us.   Long and heavy is the score.
Then cheer us for our glory now, and cheer us
    for our pain,
  And cheer us as ye never cheered before."

The folks were white and stricken, and each
    tongue seemed weighted with lead;
  Each heart was clutched in hollow hand of ice;
And every eye was staring at the horror of the
    dead,
  The pity of the men who paid the price.
They were come, were come to mock us, in the
    first flush of our peace;
  Through writhing lips their teeth were all
    agleam;

THE MARCH OF THE DEAD

They were coming in their thousands — oh,
    would they never cease!
  I closed my eyes, and then — it was a dream.

There was triumph, triumph, triumph down the
    scarlet gleaming street;
  The town was mad; a man was like a boy.
A thousand flags were flaming where the sky and
    city meet;
  A thousand bells were thundering the joy.
There was music, mirth and sunshine; but some
    eyes shone with regret;
  And while we stun with cheers our homing
    braves,
O God, in Thy great mercy, let us nevermore
    forget
  The graves they left behind, the bitter graves.

"FIGHTING MAC"

A LIFE TRAGEDY

A pistol shot rings round and round the world;
   In pitiful defeat a warrior lies.
A last defiance to dark Death is hurled,
   A last wild challenge shocks the sunlit skies.
   Alone he falls, with wide, wan, woeful eyes:
Eyes that could smile at death — could not face
      shame.

Alone, alone he paced his narrow room,
   In the bright sunshine of that Paris day;
Saw in his thought the awful hand of doom;
   Saw in his dream his glory pass away;
   Tried in his heart, his weary heart, to pray:
"O God! who made me, give me strength to
      face
The spectre of this bitter, black disgrace."

   *   *   *   *   *   *

"FIGHTING MAC"

The burn brawls darkly down the shaggy
    glen;
  The bee-kissed heather blooms around the
    door;
He sees himself a barefoot boy again,
  Bending o'er page of legendary lore.
  He hears the pibroch, grips the red clay-
    more,
Runs with the Fiery Cross, a clansman true,
Sworn kinsman of Rob Roy and Roderick
  Dhu.

Eating his heart out with a wild desire,
  One day, behind his counter trim and
    neat,
He hears a sound that sets his brain afire —
  The Highlanders are marching down the
    street.
  Oh, how the pipes shrill out, the mad drums
    beat!
" On to the gates of Hell, my Gordons gay! "
He flings his hated yardstick away.

"FIGHTING MAC"

He sees the sullen pass, high-crowned with
    snow,
    Where Afghans cower with eyes of gleaming
    hate.
He hurls himself against the hidden foe.
    They try to rally — ah, too late, too late!
    Again, defenseless, with fierce eyes that wait
For death, he stands, like baited bull at bay,
And flouts the Boers, that mad Majuba day.

He sees again the murderous Soudan,
    Blood-slaked and rapine-swept. He seems
    to stand
Upon the gory plain of Omdurman.
    Then Magersfontein, and supreme command
    Over his Highlanders. To shake his hand
A King is proud, and princes call him friend.
And glory crowns his life — and now the end,

The awful end. His eyes are dark with doom;
    He hears the shrapnel shrieking overhead;
He sees the ravaged ranks, the flame-stabbed
    gloom.

" FIGHTING MAC "

Oh, to have fallen! — the battle-field his bed,
With Wauchope and his glorious brother-
    dead.
Why was he saved for this, for this?   And now
He raises the revolver to his brow.

       *   *   *   *   *   *

In many a Highland home, framed with rude
    art,
  You'll find his portrait, rough-hewn, stern and
    square;
It's graven in the Fuyam fellah's heart;
  The Ghurka reads it at his evening prayer;
  The raw lands know it, where the fierce suns
    glare;
The Dervish fears it.   Honor to his name
Who holds aloft the shield of England's fame.

Mourn for our hero, men of Northern race!
  We do not know his sin; we only know
His sword was keen. He laughed death in the
    face,
  And struck, for Empire's sake, a giant blow.

" FIGHTING MAC "

His arm was strong.   Ah! well they learnt,
     the foe
The echo of his deeds is ringing yet —
Will ring for aye.   All else . . . let us forget.

THE WOMAN AND THE ANGEL

An angel was tired of heaven, as he lounged in
 the golden street;
His halo was tilted sideways, and his harp lay
 mute at his feet;
So the Master stooped in His pity, and gave him
 a pass to go,
For the space of a moon, to the earth-world, to
 mix with the men below.

He doffed his celestial garments, scarce waiting
 to lay them straight;
He bade good by to Peter, who stood by the
 golden gate;
The sexless singers of heaven chanted a fond
 farewell,
And the imps looked up as they pattered on the
 red-hot flags of hell.

THE WOMAN AND THE ANGEL

Never was seen such an angel — eyes of
    heavenly blue,
Features that shamed Apollo, hair of a golden
    hue;
The women simply adored him; his lips were
    like Cupid's bow;
But he never ventured to use them — and so
    they voted him slow.

Till at last there came One Woman, a marvel
    of loveliness,
And she whispered to him: " Do you love me? "
       And he answered that woman, " Yes."
And she said: " Put your arms around me, and
    kiss me, and hold me — so —"
But fiercely he drew back, saying: " This thing
    is wrong, and I know."

Then sweetly she mocked his scruples, and softly
    she him beguiled:
" You, who are verily man among men, speak
    with the tongue of a child.

THE WOMAN AND THE ANGEL

We have outlived the old standards; we have
    burst, like an over-tight thong,
The ancient, outworn, Puritanic traditions of
    Right and Wrong."

Then the Master feared for His angel, and
    called him again to His side,
For oh, the woman was wondrous, and oh, the
    angel was tried!
And deep in his hell sang the Devil, and this
    was the strain of his song:
" The ancient, outworn, Puritanic traditions of
    Right and Wrong."

THE RHYME OF THE RESTLESS ONES

We couldn't sit and study for the law;
  The stagnation of a bank we couldn't stand;
For our riot blood was surging, and we didn't
      need much urging
  To excitements and excesses that are banned.
So we took to wine and drink and other things,
  And the devil in us struggled to be free;
Till our friends rose up in wrath, and they
      pointed out the path,
  And they paid our debts and packed us o'er
      the sea.

Oh, they shook us off and shipped us o'er the
      foam,
To the larger lands that lure a man to roam;
      And we took the chance they gave
      Of a far and foreign grave,
And we bade good-by for evermore to home.

RHYME OF THE RESTLESS ONES

And some of us are climbing on the peak,
   And some of us are camping on the plain;
By pine and palm you'll find us, with never claim
      to bind us,
   By track and trail you'll meet us once again.

We are fated serfs to freedom — sky and sea;
   We have failed where slummy cities overflow;
But the stranger ways of earth know our pride
      and know our worth,
   And we go into the dark as fighters go.

Yes, we go into the night as brave men go,
Though our faces they be often streaked with
      woe;
   Yet we're hard as cats to kill,
   And our hearts are reckless still,
And we've danced with death a dozen times or
      so.

And you'll find us in Alaska after gold,
   And you'll find us herding cattle in the South.

RHYME OF THE RESTLESS ONES

We like strong drink and fun, and, when the
        race is run,
  We often die with curses in our mouth.
We are wild as colts unbroke, but never mean.
    Of our sins we've shoulders broad to bear the
        blame;
But we'll never stay in town and we'll never
        settle down,
  And we'll never have an object or an aim.

No, there's that in us that time can never tame;
And life will always seem a careless game;
    And they'd better far forget —
    Those who say they love us yet —
Forget, blot out with bitterness our name.

NEW YEAR'S EVE

It's cruel cold on the water-front, silent and
    dark and drear;
  Only the black tide weltering, only the hissing
    snow;
And I, alone, like a storm-tossed wreck, on this
    night of the glad New Year,
  Shuffling along in the icy wind, ghastly and
    gaunt and slow.

They're playing a tune in McGuffy's saloon, and
    it's cheery and bright in there
  (God! but I'm weak — since the bitter dawn,
    and never a bite of food);
I'll just go over and slip inside — I mustn't give
    way to despair —
  Perhaps I can bum a little booze if the boys
    are feeling good.

NEW YEAR'S EVE

They'll jeer at me, and they'll sneer at me, and
      they'll call me a whiskey soak;
  (" Have a drink?   Well, thankee kindly, sir,
      I don't mind if I do.")
A drivelling, dirty, gin-joint fiend, the butt of the
      bar-room joke;
  Sunk and sodden and hopeless —" Another?
      Well, here's to you! "

McGuffy is showing a bunch of the boys how
      Bob Fitzsimmons hit;
  The barman is talking of Tammany Hall,
      and why the ward boss got fired.
I'll just sneak into a corner and they'll let me
      alone a bit;
  The room is reeling round and round . . .
      O God! but I'm tired, I'm tired. . . .

*   *   *   *   *   *

Roses she wore on her breast that night.   Oh,
      but their scent was sweet!
  Alone we sat on the balcony, and the fan-
      palms arched above;

NEW YEAR'S EVE

The witching strain of a waltz by Strauss came
  up to our cool retreat,
 And I prisoned her little hand in mine, and
  I whispered my plea of love.

Then sudden the laughter died on her lips, and
  lowly she bent her head;
And oh, there came in the deep, dark eyes a
  look that was heaven to see;
And the moments went, and I waited there, and
  never a word was said,
 And she plucked from her bosom a rose of
  red and shyly gave it to me.

Then the music swelled to a crash of joy, and
  the lights blazed up like day,
 And I held her fast to my throbbing heart,
  and I kissed her bonny brow.
" She is mine, she is mine for evermore! " the
  violins seemed to say,
 And the bells were ringing the New Year in
  — O God! I can hear them now.

NEW YEAR'S EVE

Don't you remember that long, last waltz, with
 its sobbing, sad refrain?
 Don't you remember that last good-by, and
  the dear eyes dim with tears?
Don't you remember that golden dream, with
 never a hint of pain,
 Of lives that would blend like an angel-song
  in the bliss of the coming years?

Oh, what have I lost! What have I lost!
 Ethel, forgive, forgive!
 The red, red rose is faded now, and it's fifty
  years ago.
'Twere better to die a thousand deaths than live
 each day as I live!
 I have sinned, I have sunk to the lowest
  depths — but oh, I have suffered so!

Hark! Oh, hark! I can hear the bells! . . .
 Look! I can see her there,
 Fair as a dream . . . but it fades . . . And
  now — I can hear the dreadful hum

113

NEW YEAR'S EVE

Of the crowded court . . . See! the Judge
    looks down . . . NOT GUILTY, my
    Lord, I swear . . .
  The bells — I can hear the bells again! . . .
    Ethel, I come, I come! . . .

    *   *   *   *   *   *

" Rouse up, old man, it's twelve o'clock. You
    can't sleep here, you know.
  Say! ain't you got no sentiment? Lift up
    your muddled head;
Have a drink to the glad New Year, a drop
    before you go —
  You darned old dirty hobo . . . My God!
    Here, boys! He's DEAD! "

COMFORT

Say! You've struck a heap of trouble —
    Bust in business, lost your wife;
No one cares a cent about you,
    You don't care a cent for life;
Hard luck has of hope bereft you,
    Health is failing, wish you'd die —
Why, you've still the sunshine left you
    And the big, blue sky.

Sky so blue it makes you wonder
    If it's heaven shining through;
Earth so smiling 'way out yonder,
    Sun so bright it dazzles you;
Birds a-singing, flowers a-flinging
    All their fragrance on the breeze;
Dancing shadows, green, still meadows —
    Don't you mope, you've still got these.

COMFORT

These, and none can take them from you;
   These, and none can weigh their worth.
What! you're tired and broke and beaten? —
   Why, you're rich — you've got the earth!
Yes, if you're a tramp in tatters,
   While the blue sky bends above
You've got nearly all that matters —
   You've got God, and God is love.

THE HARPY

There was a woman, and she was wise; woefully
    wise was she;
She was old, so old, yet her years all told were
    but a score and three;
And she knew by heart, from finish to start, the
    Book of Iniquity.

There is no hope for such as I on earth, nor yet
    in Heaven;
Unloved I live, unloved I die, unpitied, unfor-
    given;
A loathèd jade, I ply my trade, unhallowed and
    unshriven.

THE HARPY

I paint my cheeks, for they are white, and cheeks
    of chalk men hate;
Mine eyes with wine I make them shine, that
    man may seek and sate;
With overhead a lamp of red I sit me down and
    wait

Until they come, the nightly scum, with drunken
    eyes aflame;
Your sweethearts, sons, ye scornful ones —'tis
    I who know their shame.
The gods, ye see, are brutes to me — and so I
    play my game.

For life is not the thing we thought, and not the
    thing we plan;
And Woman in a bitter world must do the best
    she can —
Must yield the stroke, and bear the yoke, and
    serve the will of man;

THE HARPY

Must serve his need and ever feed the flame of
    his desire,
Though be she loved for love alone, or be she
    loved for hire;
For every man since life began is tainted with
    the mire.

And though you know he love you so and set
    you on love's throne;
Yet let your eyes but mock his sighs, and let
    your heart be stone,
Lest you be left (as I was left) attainted and
    alone.

From love's close kiss to hell's abyss is one sheer
    flight, I trow,
And wedding ring and bridal bell are will-o'-
    wisps of woe,
And 'tis not wise to love too well, and this all
    women know.

THE HARPY

Wherefore, the wolf-pack having gorged upon
      the lamb, their prey,
With siren smile and serpent guile I make the
      wolf-pack pay —
With velvet paws and flensing claws, a tigress
      roused to slay.

One who in youth sought truest truth and found
      a devil's lies;
A symbol of the sin of man, a human sacrifice.
Yet shall I blame on man the shame? Could it
      be otherwise?

Was I not born to walk in scorn where others
      walk in pride?
The Maker marred, and, evil-starred, I drift
      upon His tide;
And He alone shall judge His own, so I His
      judgment bide.

THE HARPY

Fate has written a tragedy; its name is " The Human Heart."
The Theatre is the House of Life, Woman the mummer's part;
The Devil enters the prompter's box and the play is ready to start.

PREMONITION

'Twas a year ago and the moon was bright
  (Oh, I remember so well, so well) ;
I walked with my love in a sea of light,
    And the voice of my sweet was a silver bell.
      And sudden the moon grew strangely dull,
        And sudden my love had taken wing;
      I looked on the face of a grinning skull,
        I strained to my heart a ghastly thing.

'Twas but fantasy, for my love lay still
  In my arms, with her tender eyes aglow,
And she wondered why my lips were chill,
    Why I was silent and kissed her so.
      A year has gone and the moon is bright,
        A gibbous moon, like a ghost of woe;
      I sit by a new-made grave to-night,
        And my heart is broken — it's strange,
        you know.

THE TRAMPS

Can you recall, dear comrade, when we tramped
  God's land together,
 And we sang the old, old Earth-song, for our
  youth was very sweet;
When we drank and fought and lusted, as we
  mocked at tie and tether,
 Along the road to Anywhere, the wide world
  at our feet —

Along the road to Anywhere, when each day
  had its story;
 When time was yet our vassal, and life's jest
  was still unstale;
When peace unfathomed filled our hearts as,
  bathed in amber glory,
 Along the road to Anywhere we watched the
  sunsets pale?

THE TRAMPS

Alas! the road to Anywhere is pitfalled with
    disaster;
  There's hunger, want, and weariness, yet O
    we loved it so!
As on we tramped exultantly, and no man was
    our master,
  And no man guessed what dreams were ours,
    as, swinging heel and toe,
We tramped the road to Anywhere, the magic
    road to Anywhere,
  The tragic road to Anywhere, such dear, dim
    years ago.

L'ENVOI

You who have lived in the land,
You who have trusted the trail,
You who are strong to withstand,
You who are swift to assail:
Songs have I sung to beguile,
Vintage of desperate years,
Hard as a harlot's smile,
Bitter as unshed tears.

Little of joy or mirth,
Little of ease I sing;
Sagas of men of earth
Humanly suffering,
Such as you all have done;
Savagely faring forth,
Sons of the midnight sun,
Argonauts of the North.

125

L'ENVOI

Far in the land God forgot
  Glimmers the lure of your trail;
Still in your lust are you taught
  Even to win is to fail.
    Still you must follow and fight
      Under the vampire wing;
    There in the long, long night
      Hoping and vanquishing.

Husbandman of the Wild,
  Reaping a barren gain;
Scourged by desire, reconciled
  Unto disaster and pain;
    These, my songs, are for you,
      You who are seared with the brand.
    God knows I have tried to be true;
      Please God you will understand.